THAT'S THE JOB FOR ME!

I'M GOING TO BE A TEACHER!

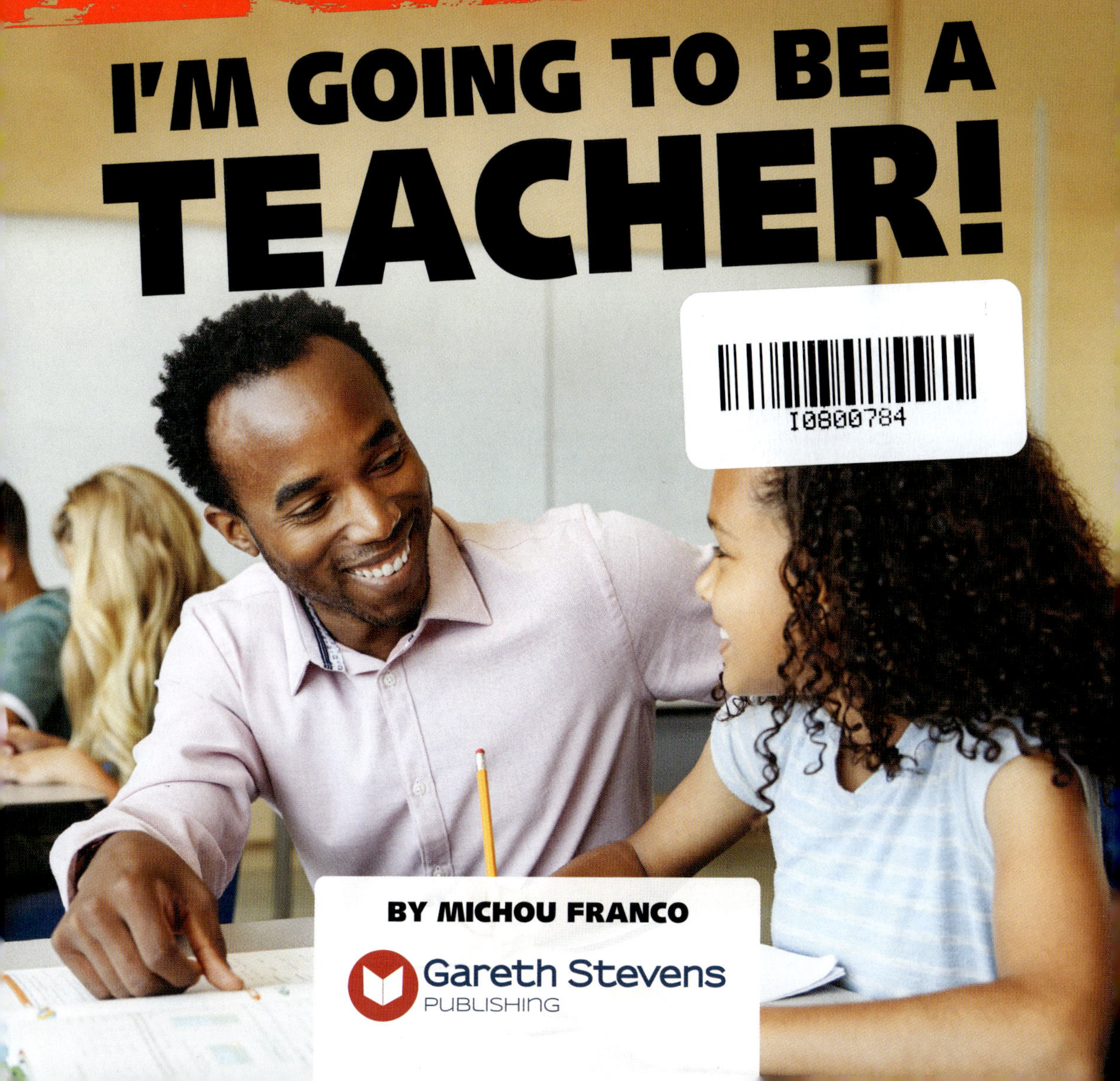

BY MICHOU FRANCO

Gareth Stevens PUBLISHING

Please visit our website, www.garethstevens.com. For a free color catalog of all our high-quality books, call toll free 1-800-542-2595 or fax 1-877-542-2596.

Library of Congress Cataloging-in-Publication Data

Names: Franco, Michou, author.
Title: I'm going to be a teacher! / Michou Franco.
Description: Buffalo, NY : Gareth Stevens Publishing, 2025. | Series: That's the job for me! | Includes bibliographical references and index.
Identifiers: LCCN 2023037612 (print) | LCCN 2023037613 (ebook) | ISBN 9781538293355 (library binding) | ISBN 9781538293348 (paperback) | ISBN 9781538293362 (ebook)
Subjects: LCSH: Teachers–Juvenile literature. | Teaching–Juvenile literature.
Classification: LCC LB1775 .F725 2025 (print) | LCC LB1775 (ebook) | DDC 371.1–dc23/eng/20230906
LC record available at https://lccn.loc.gov/2023037612
LC ebook record available at https://lccn.loc.gov/2023037613

Published in 2025 by
Gareth Stevens Publishing
2544 Clinton Street
Buffalo, NY 14224

Designer: Claire Zimmermann
Editor: Therese Shea

Photo credits: Cover, pp. 1, 7, 19 Monkey Business Images/Shutterstock.com; Series Art (background) Salmanalfa/Shutterstock.com; p. 5 gorillaimages/Shutterstock.com; p. 9 Drazen Zigic/Shutterstock.com; p. 11 Asia Images Group/Shutterstock.com; p. 13 wavebreakmedia/Shutterstock.com; p. 15 AVAVA/Shutterstock.com; p. 17 Rawpixel.com/Shutterstock.com; p. 21 antoniodiaz/Shutterstock.com.

Printed in the United States of America

CPSIA compliance information: Batch #CS25GS: For further information contact Gareth Stevens, New York, New York at 1-800-542-2595.

CONTENTS

Boldface words appear in the glossary.

Future Teacher

I love to read and write. I love to learn too. And I *really* love to share what I learn. So, I'm going to be a teacher. I practice a lot! When I'm older, I'll decide what kind of teacher to be.

1 2 3

Choosing a Path

Some teachers teach young children. Some teach older students. And others teach those in between! Some teachers teach one grade, such as kindergarten. Others teach one **subject**, such as math. They may teach the subject to several grades.

THE WORLD MAP

School First

Most teachers go to **college**. That's often four years of study. In college, some study how to be teachers. Others study a subject, such as history or English. Then, they take more classes that train them to become teachers.

Student Teachers

People studying to become teachers are called student teachers. They spend time in a classroom. They watch teachers who have **experience**. They practice teaching the class. Student teachers must pass exams, or tests, too. Finally, they receive a teaching **certificate**.

Which Certificate?

A teaching certificate says a teacher is **qualified** to teach in a preschool, **elementary school**, middle school, or high school. For older grades, the certificate may be for a certain subject. Gym teachers, art teachers, and others need to have special teaching certificates too.

More Than Teaching

Teachers teach, but they also do other kinds of work. They make **lesson** plans for each day. These plans may change because some students learn in different ways. Teachers also grade homework and tests. Grades tell teachers how well their students are learning.

Meetings

Teachers make time to meet with students who need extra help. They may meet with parents and caregivers so they can work together to help a student. They also meet with other teachers and school workers. They plan special events for the whole school.

Teachers' Features

Teachers need certain skills. They need to be good speakers and good listeners. They must be able to adapt. That means change their way of doing things. This can help their students learn. Teachers must be **patient** and try to understand their students.

Still Learning

Many teachers continue to learn after their training is done. They take classes to find new ways of teaching. They learn more about the subjects they teach too. Good teachers are always trying to be better teachers. I can't wait to be a teacher!

Output
3K
555
npn
distance: ",
n);
3- Print 3D
4- Wire sch
5- Test
6- Write code

GLOSSARY

certificate: A document, or official paper, that is proof that someone has completed a school or training program.

college: A school after high school.

elementary school: In the United States, a school for young children.

experience: Skills gained by doing something.

lesson: A part of a class intended to teach something.

patient: Able to wait a long time without becoming upset.

qualified: Having the skill, experience, or knowledge to do a job.

subject: An area of knowledge in school.